Close With Your Open

THE PITCHFREAKS GUIDE TO 10 SECOND PITCHES THAT SELL

Antonio White

Pitchfreaks
PRESS

Pitchfreaks Press

Copyright © 2020 by Antonio White, Pitchfreaks, Inc.
All Rights Reserved.

No portion of this book may be reproduced in any form or by any means (which includes mechanically, electronically, or by any other means, including photocopying), without written permission from the author. Permission should be addressed in writing to support@pitchfreaks.com

This book is designed to provide entertainment to readers. It is shared and sold with the understanding the author isn't engaged to render any type of psychological, medical, legal or any other kind of personal or professional advice. No warranties or guarantees are expressed or implied by the author's choice to include any of the content in this volume. The reader should always consult qualified professional advisors before adopting any of the suggestions in this book or drawing any ideas, inferences or practices from this book. The author shall not be liable for any physical, psychological, emotional, financial, material, or commercial damages, including, but not limited to, special, incidental, consequential or other damages. There is no such thing as getting rich quickly. Reported results are not typical. The reader is responsible for their own choices, actions and results.

ISBN: 978-1-7351342-0-8

Editor: Christina White
Book Design: Christina White
Cover Design, Cartoons & Calligraphy: Antonio White
Editorial advisor: Carolyn Flowers
Editing Support: Estanislao Rodriguez, Jr. and Richard Tardif

Printed in the United States of America

To my Wife, Christina
   You are my inspiration. Thank you for your amazing love and care throughout the 9-year ordeal of making this book. This project would not have happened without your dedication, support, and patience.

To my Mother, Emily; my Father, Serge; and my Brother, John
   Thank you for your love, unwavering encouragement, and for giving me everything I needed growing up. Thank you for always having my back.

To Esther and Albert
   Thank you for making Christina!

To my Tío, Estanislao
   Thanks to you and Uncle Jerry for a lifetime of love and encouragement.

*"Welcome, Pitchfreaks!
Behind this curtain, all your dreams are possible.
We're so excited for you!"*

May I be Frank?
A renowned Silicon Valley Executive and Investor offers a rather forward *Foreword*

pg 2

The Origin.
Do you like to know how the sausage is made? Grab a bite of this *Preface*

pg 4

Curious Minded?
If you're curious of how a "Wild and Crazy Guy", a "Mad Man", and a YouTube Algorithm set me on this path, journey to the *Introduction*

pg 11

Love Selling?
If you hate selling, you're going to LOVE this chapter. (If you love selling, you're going to LOOOOOOOOOVE this chapter)—Visit *Chapter 1: The 3 Step Winning Pitch*

pg 18

Mindreading 101.
Would you love the chance to fuse your brain with your customer's and know exactly what to say during your pitch to stack the deck in your favor?—Check out *Chapter 2: Articulating Your Value from Your Prospect's Perspective*

pg 27

Instant IQ Hack!

Want your prospects to think you're a genius? This essential skill is the single easiest way to establish yourself as an authority in the mind of your audience—Jump to *Exercise 1: Identifying Your Value*

pg 34

Fear vs. Joy—Answered!

This is the chapter THEY don't want you to read. Why? Because if you incorporate emotion into your pitch, THEY will have to dig into their profits to compete—Journey to *Chapter 3: How to Incorporate Emotion into Your Pitch*

pg 41

Finding Your Emote Control.

Want to send your competition crying home to their Momma? Don't skip this exercise. In the business of pitching, the one who can connect deepest emotionally—wins! *Exercise 2: Adding Emotion into Your Pitch*

pg 46

Guilt-Free, Party Crashing!

Do you get squeamish about closing? If so, you're going to LOVE this chapter. (If you're a closing-machine, you're going to LOOOOOOOOOVE this chapter). RSVP to *Chapter 4: The Invitation, Your Friendly Call to Action*

pg 56

—Speaking of Segues...

If you're lacking a great transition from your customer greeting into your product or service demo, this is the exercise you've been waiting for. Interested? Go to ***Exercise 3: Offering a Customer Invitation (Call to Action)***

pg 61

Your Pitch—*Presto!*

Do you love magic? This chapter's exercises reveal your pitch like—Presto! Make your dreams a reality—vanish to ***Chapter 5: Putting It All Together***

pg 67

Would You Like Fries With That?

Ever wish that you had a pitch, so smooth, it would make people jealous? This is where we assemble all the pieces and make your wish come true! Slide to ***Exercise 4: Complete Your First Draft***

pg 69

...One More Thing...

Want your pitch to shine so bright you can see it from Jupiter? This is where all your brilliant work– quite literally–pays off! Blast off to ***Exercise 5: Writing Your Final Draft***

pg 77

Come Join the Party
Are you looking for a community of other Pitchfreaks to practice your pitch with? Want to connect and grow with other pitch pros? See *Afterward*

pg 86

Gratitude[2]
If you're looking for some gratitude, this is where you'll find it. Humbly submitted on *Acknowledgement*

pg 89

Getting Personal
A bit more info on the author to quell your curiosity. Peek on *About the Author*

pg 90

Humanity has not taken a single action, since the dawn of civilization, without being sold on a pitch.

What to eat, where to live, who to love, who to hate, waging war or seeking peace—all of these decisions—and more, are based upon you buying someone else's pitch.

The most powerful pitch in life is the one you sell yourself.

—The Pitchfreak, Antonio White

Forward
By Scott Eagle
Veteran Silicon Valley Executive and Investor

Wow, a forward from Scott Eagle. I know you don't want to miss a word!

OK, seriously, I am not Steven King, nor I am not Elon Musk, and frankly, I can't hold a candle to Kim Kardashian for pitching stuff. Sorry. But I have been successful in my career in selling my ideas, vision and businesses using principles that are in this book, and so hopefully that buys me a modicum of credibility.

Please note that I am not a fan of pedestrian self-help books, or publications that pontificate about the 'ideal' way to deal with adversarial or tough business issues. Nor am I fan of the majority of negotiation-oriented books that aren't practical in the real world. That said, I am a whore for any deep and honest insights that can help me develop win-win relationships in business and in life. (Maybe whore isn't the best word, and my mama will slap me, but you get the point – I have a passionate relationship with any value proposition that can help me be successful in life).

That is why I am so honored to write this brief blurb for *Close with Your Open*. Antonio White has broken through the noise on the topic of pitch negotiations in a straightforward (and profound way). And yes, to be upfront, Antonio has been a friend, a consultant to me over the years and an amazing sounding board for all my good/bad ideas – but I wouldn't be writing this if I didn't honestly think that this book could change your life. And it could, if you pay attention and follow some of the key pitch principles.

OK, calling bullshit on myself. Honestly, I don't think that a single book can really change your life. But yes, I do believe that a single book can open up your mind to the possibilities of the success you could have. And a single book can give you tips, insights and more importantly, inspiration for you to change the world. One pitch at a time. Really.

So please take the time to really read *Close with Your Open* and assimilate the key principles. Challenge the areas you disagree with and embrace the rest of the brilliance. And there is much brilliance here. And remember, as you pitch your ideas, consider what Mark Twain said – "It's not the size of the dog in the fight, it's the size of the fight in the dog". So, believe in yourself, follow Antonio's guidelines, and fight to get what you want and be passionate in your pitch. It will pay off!

Pitch on, fellow freaks,

Scott

Preface

Welcome Pitchfreaks!

So, where did this whole idea of the *Close with Your Open* and the 3-Step Winning Pitch Framework come from? One of my key inspirations for the concept came from attending the VidSummit Conference in 2019 founded by a great mentor of mine, the preeminent YouTube™ strategist, Derral Eves.

At the event, Karen Kavett, a YouTuber and Designer in charge of creating all thumbnails for YouTube Originals series, along with Ali Jardine, Channel Strategist, reported that a large data analysis of viewers who clicked on YouTube™ thumbnails revealed that 20% of those people abandoned their selection within the first 10 seconds of watching it– some abandoned the video as soon as two and a half seconds. In case you're guessing *clickbait* was the culprit—guess again!

With millions of YouTube™ videos to choose from on the platform, if viewers didn't immediately see what they expected after clicking the thumbnail, they moved on. This became the cornerstone for developing my program.

Too many entrepreneurs choose to slowly build up evidence of value in their pitch decks and customer sales presentations—*all too often boring viewers to tears* long before getting to the conclusion of their presentation. Don't believe me? Ask yourself how many times you've started rolling your eyes within moments of someone *cluelessly* presenting to you?—*Wait! Are you rolling your eyes at me right now!* ;-)

In recent years, startup accelerators such as the technology-focused, Y Combinator (YC), have offered new founders training in their pitch deck building skills, in hopes that learning from successful companies that have closed investor rounds would share their insights into creating effective pitch decks. Unfortunately, outside of Silicon Valley, there is still far too little access to instruction or mentorship on the topic—not to mention that YC to date is focused primarily on Software as a Service (SAAS) startups. That means if you're a widget-maker or cancer-curer, your options in finding credible pitch development guidance is limited.

Why is this a big deal? Well if people are abandoning YouTube™ videos within the first 10 seconds because they're not finding what they're looking for, then whoever made those videos has missed an opportunity to share those ideas. As a result, their hard work would have been wasted for at least 20% of the people who clicked their thumbnail.

From here, an idea began brewing...*the introduction of the video* must immediately meet the expectations from the thumbnail, which needs to match expectations set by the headline, so people know they're watching the right video and don't abandon it. *If you don't capture people's attention within the first 10 seconds, you risk that 20% of people will never make it to the end of your presentation.*

The Birth of the 10 Second Pitch

This was a light bulb moment! If this could be applied to sales, particularly, to the introduction of a sales conversation, then improving the introduction of the pitch could drive greater engagement and closing opportunities for any given sales presentation.

For instance, if you are delivering a three-minute sales presentation, you should focus your greatest efforts on the first 10 seconds (30 words) of your pitch. There is a distinction made in this book between *pitch*, *sale*, and *close*. You've got your *pitch* (your sales presentation introduction or "open"), your *sale* represents the entirety of your presentation (from beginning to end), and your *close* (the acceptance and transfer of value from the prospect to the seller in exchange for delivery of the offer).

In any sales presentation you'll have prospect qualification, questions, complaints, and objections in between the open and close of a sales presentation, however, the pitch is *the big idea* or *key concept* of your presentation. In this book, you're guided to present your big idea in the first 10 seconds. Then, with your prospect's cooperation, you can proceed to a demonstration. This would ideally be followed by your prospect's agreement to buy, or "close" the deal.

The Mission Pitch

Every sale is a mission and every mission requires a Mission Pitch.

Regardless of the amount of time allocated for your presentation, your mission-pitch should only be 10 seconds. The reason why it should be 10 seconds is based upon the verified *YouTube Audience Retention Report by Visible Measures* and reported by *AdAge*, indicating that 20% of people surveyed, abandoned YouTube videos they selected within the first 10 seconds of selecting them.

> **The Lesson?** Give your prospects what they want at the beginning of your pitch or risk never getting them to your close.

Working with others in developing the framework

It doesn't matter what level of experience a person has, or which industry they work, the 3-Step Winning Pitch Framework can be applied successfully.

Imagine the *ideal* sales presentation. The ideal sales presentation would be saying "Hello," and the other person would immediately fork over the dough, right? Imagine people begging to be your customer. Imagine people throwing themselves at you to be engaged in whatever you happen to sell.

I've been involved with very sophisticated, high-stakes pitches for over 25 years and the idea that I could boil down the requirements of a winning pitch into 3-steps was previously unimaginable to me. However, after years of failed results—in one, all-night creative burst, I took a last, desperate stab at rethinking my own process. I had already provided hundreds of hours of training and testing for small business owners, but I didn't have the right framework that *took me out of the loop*. I needed a program to help people solve their pitch challenges *themselves*.

I was determined because these problems just keep repeating for people—and they're basic, rudimentary problems. I thought, if I could help people come up with a framework for handling a basic pitch, then I could help them increase the effectiveness of the other parts of their sales process.

For example, with the right framework, it would be easier for people to get early seed money investment. It would be easier for them to get angel investment. It would be easier for them to get venture capital funding. It would be easier for them to get early adopters, key new customers, or bring on important partners or employees.

If people could optimize the first 10-seconds of their pitch, they could enjoy exponential sales success by applying the framework to all of their branding and customer-facing communications.

Preface

With the specter of eight years of failure haunting me, I took a leap of faith and created the 3-Step Winning Pitch Framework. Surprisingly to me, the general outline of this program took less than four hours to complete. Well, *eight years* plus four hours!

Testing the Program Out in the Wild

I had signed up for legendary sales trainer, Grant Cardone's first mentorship program and, during a series of *Zoom* calls, it was clear that there was a need for others to be educated on pitching. As good as his mentorship was, Grant's program had nothing to offer with crafting effective mission-pitches. Since my name in the *Zoom* meeting window was "The Pitchfreak!", attendees of the calls eventually sought me out for advice. From those calls, I offered a free Pitchfreak *Zoom* call, which allowed me a real-world group to test my new program. I really thought the call was going to be a half-hour training on how to make a pitch using my new 3-Step Winning Pitch Framework.

About twenty people attended the free call and after a half hour, people became deeply engaged. We had fun and the attendees, whom I referred to as fellow Pitchfreaks, were gaining some transformative insights about pitching, sales, marketing and business. Three hours and forty-five minutes later, we were still on that first call—I realized we were on to something. I invited everyone to join me for another call for the following day. Almost everybody from the first call joined onto the second call. Others had heard through the grapevine about the call and asked to join in—this second call lasted *four* hours.

Altogether, I conducted a total of five calls, totaling 21 hours of training based upon a framework that I thought would only take 30 minutes to teach. *The last call of the sessions lasted five hours straight with no break!*

The amount of time spent teaching the framework had nothing to do with the intelligence or experience of the people on the calls, it had to do with the complexity they found in making decisions to communicate the value of their business to people.

Describing the value of an offer was the number one issue I witnessed in spending time to help people figure out who their customers were, how to articulate their message, what's important to their customers, how to add emotion, and how to have a compelling call to action.

Speaking of invitational calls to action, I'd love to share a couple of fun stories about how a "Jerk" and "Mad Man" taught me to sharpen my pitch skills. To learn more, continue to the *Introduction*, and let's keep this party going!

Introduction

What can Comedy Super-freak, Steve Martin and a former British Intelligence Officer, who lived in a peach-colored castle teach you about Pitching? Their tricks for instant audience engagement can be easily applied to increase your sales. To learn more, keep reading.

You have just been *pitched!*

If you're hungry for greater profits, there is no technology nor business practice available today that can deliver you a faster and less costly bottom-line result than optimizing your sales pitch. I'd love to show you how I can deliver on this, if you'd like to see?"

You have just been pitched—*again!*

In this book, a Pitch is defined as the introduction made at the beginning of a sale that is meant to open a customer's mind to learn more about your offer. You can call the whole sales presentation a pitch, but this book covers the very beginning of a pitch that will be referred to as "the Open".

It's the Pitchfreak philosophy that too many sales fail because people construct their presentations backward. After 25 years of my engagement in high-stakes presentations, marketing programs, product, service, and business launches, it's abundantly clear: *people don't spend enough time on the introduction* to their offer because they're *too focused on the end* of their sales presentation where they attempt to close the sale.

What's important to consider is the more experienced and successful the salesperson, the more likely they will focus on the "*Open*" of their pitch (even if they don't refer to it as such). Conversely newer, less experienced salespeople will more likely focus on the "*Close*".

Some salespeople think of selling as a "numbers game". To a degree that's true, because you need many people in your pipeline to sell, yet many salespeople churn through prospects at an alarming rate, not giving enough consideration to the quality of those interactions.

Increasing the quality of your sales interactions is *the* core focus of this guide. When you get this right, the money follows.

A "Wild and Crazy" Closer

A joke is a sales pitch. You either buy a joke and laugh or you don't. Just like any salesperson, a comedian either delivers the goods or they bomb. Just like a top performing sales pro, a headlining comedian needs to be exceptionally skilled at closing deals (with each joke being its own micro deal). If you can close enough "deals" over a lifetime, like Steve Martin, you become a comedy legend. In Steve Martin's Comedy course on Masterclass.com, he teaches *not to waste your introduction*. He discusses the idea between amateur, professional and seasoned comedians. The amateur comedian wastes a lot of time at the beginning of their comedy routine. When they take the stage, they spend time thanking the

Introduction

person who introduced them, the audience, they ask, "How is everyone?" and, "What's happening, (City, State, Region)? Steve Martin thinks this is a wasted opportunity. He believes the first words out of a comedian's mouth sets the tone for their entire routine, and that the anticipation is never going to be higher than just before the comedian's first spoken words.

Steve Martin states, "When you begin [your act], you should come out with a great joke right away and win the audience to make sure they're laughing, which sets up the entire performance. Don't waste your introduction. Make sure they're laughing right away, and the rest of your performance will be terrific!"

My letter from an original "Mad Man"

I was only 18 years old when I sent David Ogilvy a package featuring three of my best advertisements of the day—along with a request for him to be my mentor. If you're not familiar with Mr. Ogilvy, he was the chairman of Ogilvy and Mather, an iconic advertising agency. If you've heard of the show *Mad Men*, David Ogilvy was referenced in many episodes. He is among the founding architects of modern advertising.

David Ogilvy sent a return correspondence to me in the form of a note sheet on peach parchment, the color of his famed castle, Château de Touffou, in France. In the letter, dictated to his assistant, he explained that he didn't have time to be my mentor. He wrote me back, (I'm paraphrasing), *Hey kid, I'm a bit busy running a global company with thousands of employees!*

Thankfully, he did take time to offer me two pieces of advice of which I'll share one:

> ***"The headlines of your ads would perform better if they promised the reader a benefit." — David Ogilvy***

If you haven't read Ogilvy's famous book, *Ogilvy on Advertising*, you absolutely should. In it he states that headlines account for more than 50% engagement of any advertisement.

My three major influencers in arriving at the concept of the 3-Step Winning Pitch Framework: Ogilvy, Martin, and my YouTube mentor, Derral Eves:

David Ogilvy said: "50% percent of your advertisement's success is based upon the power of your headline."

Steve Martin said: "don't waste your introduction; the first few words out of your mouth are the most powerful for your entire show."

My VidSummit pals reported, "20% percent of people leave your YouTube video within the first ten seconds of clicking a thumbnail".

Introduction

These three statements support my premise that, firstly, the introduction to your sales presentation or process is the most important. Secondly, that the span of time to focus on should be the first 10 seconds to make sure you're getting the most value and benefit from time you're investing in sales communication.

How is this basic, rudimentary pitch going to make a difference in people's lives? The short version of the story comes from my efforts to scale my own business beyond consulting for almost eight years, often asking myself how to come up with a product that isn't already available in the market?

How my own winning pitch set me free!

There is such saturation of *"Marketing Guruism"* in the marketplace. How could anyone compete when everyone is a claiming to be a marketing master? I was going to have to dig deep to stand out. Surely, if I'm able to deliver amazing results for my clients, what's stopping me for delivering for myself? Looking at myself from the outside allowed me to ask myself the same questions and dig deep to gain the same transformative insights as my clients. The result of this series of insights was my first program entitled, *10 Seconds to Live: How to Pitch Like your Life Depends on It.* It was clear that dominating *Pitching*—this specific, narrow specialty—where marketing and sales meet was (and is) the perfect niche for me. It's effective because most sales pros are horrible marketers and most marketers are horrible salespeople.

Legendary Branding pioneer, Walter Landor

said, "Branding is a promise." I'll add that branding is the promise of an experience between you and your customer." Your Pitch is the first step in the process of setting the expectation of that experience. If you're ready to get real about making a meaningful change in your profits, you came to the right place. All your marketing and sales activities can be exponentially enhanced once you understand the Pitchfreak, 3-Step Winning Pitch Framework.

Let's go, Pitchfreaks!

Within Constraint is Freedom!

Chapter One:
A Winning Pitch in 3 Steps

So, what's a "close with an open" and what are these so-called "3-Steps to a Winning Pitch?"

Closing with your open, quite literally means creating prospect interest and agreement at the very beginning (opening) of your sales pitch. If you need more explanation on this, read this book's preface. To test how engaging your pitch is right now, I offer you a simple challenge question.

If someone else was giving your pitch, word for word, would they have the same sales success as you?

If you answered, "No." or "Not sure.", then your sales success may likely benefit from your position of authority, celebrity, or personal/professional relationship with your prospects or customers. If you answered "Yes," then you're likely in one of two categories. The first category might be that you have a product that is highly desired. If so, that's awesome, you can use this system to increase your profit margins and sell even more. The second category might be that your communications employ high-pressure or tactics of questionable ethics to force or shame people into agreement. If so, *Closing with Your Open* (CWYO) may likely outperform your results and allow you to sell *shame-free*.

The 3-Step Winning Pitch Framework

Your Pitch requires the combination of *Customer Value* + *Emotion* + *Invitation* (CTA) all delivered *within 10 Seconds* (30 words or less). I like to write the framework as:

P=VEI/10sec

DO NOT BE DECEIVED BY THE SIMPLICITY OF THIS FRAMEWORK.

Just like $E=MC^2$, there is a lot to unpack in order to effectively apply the equation.

The delivery: Your pitch must include all three elements of the 3-Step Winning Pitch Framework AND be concluded within the first 10 seconds of your communication. 10 seconds is 30 words or less (comfortably spoken).

Step One: VALUE

Focus on the value of your product or service from the perspective of your prospect. This means you must explain how your customer receives value after they have experienced the successful effect or result of having used your product or service. Articulating your value from their perspective is essential in compelling them to listen more and engage further in your sales discussion.

Step Two: EMOTION

Incorporate the emotion of joy or relief into your pitch. While there are many emotions to consider using in your pitch, for the sake of this discussion, focus on either joy or relief. These two emotions will be easy to apply most of the time to your pitch. How do you incorporate joy and relief? I'll explain later on in this chapter.

Step Three: INVITATION
(Call to Action)

Offer your prospect a simple, friendly invitation to learn more about your offer. You want your pitch to feel and sound conversational. This does not mean you're being manipulative because you are rehearsed or practiced—it means you've put a lot of thought into it—so you save your prospect time during your presentation.

The better your pitch, the easier it's for you to deliver in a natural way and the more likely your prospect is going to feel interested and engaged. Your pitch could end, for instance, with: "I'd love to show an example, if you have a moment."

You can use any number of approaches in a conversational way. Your approach should compel somebody to whom you have offered value, to accept your offer. This is what I mean by the statement, "Your *opening* is really part of your *closing.*"

"Writing a winning pitch requires your very best marketing and sales thinking."

The Sales Mindset vs. The Service Mindset

If you can *close* with your *open*, life will be a lot easier for you. You'll spend less time applying pressure to people and more time serving them. As you become a more proficient sales professional, you'll learn that this has nothing to do with the movie, *Glengarry Glen Ross*, a film depicting two days in the lives of four desperate real estate salesmen and their high-pressure sales tactics. *Close with Your Open* is not about high-pressure tactics. It has everything to do with providing great customer service. The better service you can provide, the better experience your customer has, the more likely they will buy from you or use your services.

If you have an effective 10-second, 3-Step Winning Pitch Framework, you can succeed where others have floundered. One of the benefits of *Closing with Your Open* is the ability to charge more for your product or service. You'll command a higher margin as well. You will have more flexibility when working with your customer. You will enjoy incredible, meaningful, profound advantages in your interaction with your prospect than you would without using this framework.

Why? Because when using the 3-Step Winning Pitch Framework, you convey greater value, plus greater perceived value of your product or service simply because you are focused on the needs of the customer in a way they believe makes you an authority, or (at least) highly competent, in the offer you are presenting.

Let's recap. There are three steps to create a winning pitch: 1) articulating your value from the customer's perspective; 2) incorporating emotion (either joy or relief) and 3) a friendly, invitational call to action.

> Your customers should be the HERO of your pitch.

Chapter Two:
Articulating Your Value from Your Prospect's Perspective

The first step of articulating your value from the perspective of your prospect is to understand your prospect's mindset and what motivates them to buy. What I've discovered over my career, is that it's not always obvious. For some services or products, you might think it's obvious to understand why somebody might buy it. Some business owners think that the simple act of offering a product or service for sale should make it attractive for purchase.

Have Pitches for Gatekeepers and Decision Makers

For some people, selling requires pitching gatekeepers in order to get access to the ultimate decisionmaker. As a result, they try to gain access through the intermediary who directly affects their sale, because they can't immediately pitch directly to the final authority. In this case it's essential to remember a pitch that meets the needs of the intermediary is in order. The sales professional has two distinct pitches to make; one that appeals to the gatekeeper and the other that appeals to their boss. I mention this because too often people fumble the gatekeeper pitch by either undervaluing their role in the sales process or attempting to make a sophisticated pitch to someone who may have far less direct knowledge of the benefit provided by the product or service.

But My Product Sells Itself?

Anytime I'm told "this product sells itself," it's always a red flag for me. There is nothing that sells itself. Everything has to be sold. Ferrari has salespeople. Bars have salespeople. Savile Row suits, Harry Winston diamonds, political candidates, and even religions have salespeople (Jesus had 12 of them). You would think if something is so obviously wonderful, all you'd need to do is run ads to a landing page with a "Buy" button, right? Everything requires selling.

> *Nothing sells itself. Nothing in commerce is "self-evident".*

In the case of a commodity, you might be underestimating the necessity for you to dig inside your customer's mindset to discover why they would buy your product or service. You might not think you have a commodity in many cases, or to the degree that you do, you might think, it's obvious what you're selling. Your thought might be to simply present the information to the prospect and they'll understand. Well, if you're asking your prospective customer to decide, they're not going to spend time thinking about it and likely default to, "No."

Lazy Pitches Kill Sales

In Steve Krug's book, *Don't Make Me Think*, he writes about user interface design. The key concept of his book is to guide the reader in making their website or software application highly intuitive to use so it's obvious for the customer to know how they should move through the software's process, so they have a great user experience. The better the user experience, the less they have to think, the easier it's for them to move through the process of using the software.

If the user has to think about how to apply your product to meet their needs, it has a direct effect on their perceived value of your offer.

A great pitch doesn't require critical thinking by your prospect. It should be easily understood. In the event that your prospect has to think about what you're pitching them, they're going to immediately halt your sales process in their mind. They will start processing and evaluating whether you are a threat to them.

Skepticism is a normal human response. Even for people who are desperate to buy from you, the moment you engage in a sales process, an imaginary, invisible shield, is going to pop up for them to defend against you as a perceived threat. Even if I were to say: "Hey, I want to buy this product that you have. I'm interested. I'm a huge fan. I can't wait to own this product." As soon as you begin to offer me a sale, I'm going to wonder about you as a salesperson. First, are you going to try to take advantage of me? Second, am I getting the best price? Third, am I getting the best options? Fourth, is this the right decision for me to make? And finally, are you the right person from whom I should buy? If these questions come up from someone who wants to buy your product, imagine the questions that come up for somebody who is on the fence or somebody who, just from quickly scanning your ad, doesn't know if they need you.

Generating great customer leads is tough and expensive. Once your customer feels you're attempting to manipulate them, they immediately go on the defensive and you risk losing them. Be protective of your lead opportunities and avoid manipulative tactics of any kind.

Using your Pitch to Get to the Point

Getting to the point is essential for sales success, especially for high ticket products and services. Prospects may not cut you off due to politeness, but too often, salespeople give far too much background information before they get to the point of their sales call. This can be infuriating for a prospect with limited time. To respect your prospect's time, it's essential that you understand the singular main value that your product delivers.

Deeper Product Knowledge Builds Your Credibility with Prospects

Consider how customers use your product as well as the myriad benefits it provides them. Having first-hand knowledge of these facts provides you an advantage over other salespeople who have to get this information second-hand. This should send a clear signal to you to study your product and its use by your customers.

You cannot "wing it" and expect to have a winning pitch. Salespeople would be best served by becoming more enthusiastic students of their customer's use of their product. If you're feeling stuck in your sales progress, your level of product knowledge is something that you can control. Start having conversations with customers who have already used your product.

Start studying other customers using similar products. Interview people and how they benefit from the product. What specific meaningful benefits do they receive? Is it financial, time, health, or some kind of meaningful experience?

It's not enough to say your product saves customers time and money.

You have to explain how or why a product saves time or money and you must explain so in a simple, believable, and easily understandable manner—of course remembering you're limited to accomplish this using 30 words or less.

"A winning pitch starts with understanding your customer's view of the world."

Exercise 1: Identifying Your Value

Visit www.Pitchfreaks.com/CWYO to register and receive Free Access to the complete Exercise Guide download for this book.

Time to Complete (30 Minutes)

BEFORE YOU BEGIN: This is THE most important exercise of the series. Make certain to give yourself uninterrupted time to focus on listing as many viable benefits as possible. The subsequent lessons all build upon this exercise, remember—a spectacular performance requires spectacular preparation.

Objective: Identify and Clarify Your Product's Value from Your Prospect's Perspective

Instructions: In the Benefit Category section, indicate the type of benefit you'll explore with an "X" or checkmark. In Section A List your customer benefits, in one to three words, In Section B explain how they are achieved and in Section C identify the function or process that delivers the result. (List as many benefits in Section A as you can within 10 minutes. Afterward you have 20 minutes to fill out Sections B and C to clarify each listed benefit.

TIP: You may think your product or service offers only one type of benefit for customers, but I encourage you to consider that more than one benefit category might be possible for each benefit you list.

Be Specific: If your product saves people time, write specific ways that it saves them time. Make sure it's as descriptive as possible. It's not enough to say something saves people time, you have to prove it. You must show evidence. Explain how it saves customers time. The same applies to saving people money. If your product saves people money, describe how, in some novel way. What is it about your product that allows you to accomplish the result? Is it some function, feature, process, or framework?

Write down the function, feature, button, communication, or experience. What feature is most responsible for delivering the beneficial result? What's the singular feature or function about your product or service—it's "special sauce" or more specifically, the "core" of the special sauce that makes the results possible? Once you've completed this exercise, move on to the next chapter and explore how to incorporate *emotion* into your pitch.

REMEMBER: Make sure you don't skip any exercises as each chapter builds upon the activities from the previous chapter.

To help you along, try 10-10-10

If you're feeling stuck, my recommendation is that you focus on choosing 10 words per exercise: 10 words for the value articulation, 10 words for the emotion, and 10 words for the call to action. Go ahead, start chopping away.

Let's give it a go.

As you're going through this exercise, you might be saying, "Oh, come on man, this is just too hard. It's too hard to cut this down. I have too much to say. I have too much information I have to deliver. There's *no way* I can do it in 10 seconds."

Believe me, I've heard these comments all before. I've been crafting pitches for over 25 years. People complain that they can't come up with a simple pitch for their business for all kinds of reasons, such as:

"What I'm doing is too complicated."
"What I'm doing is too specialized."
"What I'm doing is too sophisticated."

Articulating Your Value from Your Prospect's Perspective

And in each case, when I help these clients simplify their message into 10 seconds or less... (and yes you can do this in less than 10 seconds). They are always thrilled. It can be a truly liberating feeling to have a pitch that gives you such clarity about your product or service.

In some cases, coming up with the winning pitch almost seems like magic.

My goal with this book, and with these exercises is to help you achieve a similar result as I have been able to accomplish with my clients. My intention is to take my 25 years of crafting winning pitches and transfer my knowledge to you.

If you want a better result in sales, you need a better pitch.

Exercise 1: Identifying Value

Identify and *Clarify* Your Product's Value from Your *Prospect's Perspective*

Instructions: Write in the **Product** or **Service Name** you'll be describing in this exercise. In **Section A**, list your customer benefits, in one to three words. In the **Benefit Category** section, indicate the type of benefit you'll explore with an "X" or check mark. In **Section B**, explain how the benefit is achieved. In **Section C**, identify the function or process that delivers the result. **Exercise Time: 30min.** List as many benefits as you can within 10 minutes. After listing your customer benefits, you have 20 minutes to fill out Sections B and C to clarify each benefit.

Select a *Benefit Category* for each benefit you list below.

Make certain to select a Benefit Category for each benefit. Choose the classification tied to the benefit of your customer from their perspective.

Benefit Category Legend
- **T** = Time Savings
- **M** = Money Savings
- **P** = Profit/Wealth
- **H** = Health
- **E** = Experiential (Entertainment/Spiritual)
- **F** = Functional (Skill Development)

Product or Service Name:

A. Benefit No. 1 **Benefit Category**

_____ ☐T ☐M ☐P ☐H ☐E ☐F

B. Benefit Explanation: (Explain how this benefit is achieved)

C. Function or Process: (Explain what delivers the benefit result)

A. Benefit No. 2 **Benefit Category**

_____ ☐T ☐M ☐P ☐H ☐E ☐F

B. Benefit Explanation: (Explain how this benefit is achieved)

C. Function or Process: (Explain what delivers the benefit result)

Benefits List (cont'd)

A. Benefit No. 3   **Benefit Category**
_____ ☐T ☐M ☐P ☐H ☐E ☐F

B. Benefit Explanation: (Explain how this benefit is achieved)

C. Function or Process: (Explain what delivers the benefit result)

A. Benefit No. 4   **Benefit Category**
_____ ☐T ☐M ☐P ☐H ☐E ☐F

B. Benefit Explanation: (Explain how this benefit is achieved)

C. Function or Process: (Explain what delivers the benefit result)

A. Benefit No. 5   **Benefit Category**
_____ ☐T ☐M ☐P ☐H ☐E ☐F

B. Benefit Explanation: (Explain how this benefit is achieved)

C. Function or Process: (Explain what delivers the benefit result)

A. Benefit No. 6   **Benefit Category**
_____ ☐T ☐M ☐P ☐H ☐E ☐F

B. Benefit Explanation: (Explain how this benefit is achieved)

C. Function or Process: (Explain what delivers the benefit result)

When in doubt, choose Joy.

Chapter Three:
How to Incorporate Emotion into Your Pitch

If you're reading this, it means you want to be more effective at pitching. Therefore, I implore you, if you didn't do the exercise in the previous chapter, please go complete the exercise. If you aren't able to do the exercise from the previous chapter, it'll be harder for you to do the exercise in this chapter.

If all you did was articulate your value from the perspective of your customer, you would be far ahead of most salespeople making pitches today. However, if you want to take it to the next level— if you want to really engage and connect with your prospect—there is no more powerful way than to connect *emotionally*. There are a lot of tools, techniques, processes, gimmicks, and strategies in order to artificially create emotion and compel people to make decisions based upon those emotions. Those types of tactics reduce trust in you as a sales professional. As professionals, it's essential that you work from a place of care and concern for your prospect. Applying some unethical, manipulative tactic in order to get a sale is unsustainable and only offers short-term results, while risking long-term ill will.

If you want people to be excited about employing your product or service, and you want them to be raving fans, the best way to build any long-term relationship is to treat people with respect and care—your customers are no different. The truth is, not everybody is going to be your customer, however, you still want to make sure that you are treating everyone with kindness and courtesy. Put aside the goodwill and great feelings kindness instills in those around you—anyone you meet might send you a referral or become a customer of yours in the future. While we're not going to force people to be customers by trying to manipulate them with some unethical tactic, there's nothing wrong with creating a story that connects emotionally with them.

The two emotions that I use most frequently when crafting a Pitchfreaks pitch are joy and relief.

Now, you'll see the importance of having completed Exercise 1. In that exercise you should have written a series of bullet points to articulate the value of using your product or service from your customer's perspective. With that in mind, determine, from your intuition if your product or service brings joy or relief to your customers. Go ahead and consider this now.

Does your product bring joy or relief?

Now I want you to look at your list of bullet points and determine, which of those features or functions of your product brings the most joy or the most relief to your customers? Circle the bullet points that match the corresponding emotion of your choice. In the end, you can only pick one emotion. Remember, in your final pitch you only get 30 words to complete your 10 second pitch. You only have time to pick the most important feature or function of your product that brings people *joy* or *relief*. Go ahead and decide which function/feature and emotion you'll use in crafting your pitch right now. You can always choose a different function or emotion later, but for the sake of this exercise, circle the one item from your list that brings your customers the most joy or the most relief.

Now that you've circled the feature or function bringing your customers the most value, the next step is to determine how that feature or function brings them joy or relief. Describe how your product's main function or feature achieves this result.

"Your customer's needs are often less complicated than you think."

Exercise 2: Adding Emotion to Your Pitch
Determine the emotion you'll use in your pitch.

Take one of the benefits you've chosen from *Exercise 1, Identifying Your Value*, then complete the following sentence: "My customers feel (joy or relief) after using my product or service because… (fill in the blank)".

For example. "My clients feel more joy and confidence as a result of using my 3-Step Winning Pitch Framework which allows them to connect and engage more deeply with their prospects and close more deals."

Tip: You might be confused if your product or service brings joy or relief to your customer. Don't worry about that right now. Pick the one that comes from your gut or intuition.

Write a sentence based upon the joy or relief emotion. If you're feeling the emotion you picked isn't working, then try the alternate emotion. Write how your product brings customers joy, then write how it brings relief. You might find it's possible that your product or service brings both joy and relief—and that's not unusual. The challenge though is that you only have 10 seconds to deliver this pitch, so you have to pick one. By picking joy or relief, you want to match the emotion that best articulates and highlights your value statement from the previous exercise. Here's another tip. The clue to determine if you should choose joy or relief should really be based upon the mindset of your prospect.

How to Incorporate Emotion into Your Pitch

If the mindset of your prospect is entrepreneurial, then you should consider the emotion of *joy*. If your prospect isn't entrepreneurial, then you should likely focus on the emotion of *relief*.

Pitch Variables

Ultimately, you will only know if your prospect is entrepreneurial or managerial focused based upon understanding your specific customers. Yes, it's possible that you have more than one customer type. A customer could be entrepreneurial and managerial-focused, but you should know which trait they lean towards most. If you truly have two different customer types, you can have two distinct pitches. One pitch that uses joy for the entrepreneurial-focused customer, and an alternative pitch that uses relief for the managerial-focused customer. If you're in a situation where you're talking to a large group of people and you don't know if they're entrepreneurial-focused or managerial-focused, my recommendation is to lead with the emotion of joy rather than relief. You will inspire people more. You're going to set yourself apart from other presenters who will be most likely talking about pain points and problems rather than opportunities.

If you're pitching against other people, by using joy, you're going to set yourself apart, because customers who part with their cash gravitate most often towards those who provide joyful experiences and aspirational ideas over those who emphasize pain. The reason for this is because people who are in pain already know they're in pain. If you articulate your value effectively, then you are going to demonstrate that you already know people are in pain and you have a solution. Make sense? Good! Let's keep going.

Reminder: Make sure to write at least three to five emotional statements based upon the joy and/or relief emotions.

Showcasing Your Most Valuable Asset

Think about it like this: The 10-second pitch you're showcasing is your most valuable asset. It may be the most valuable asset you will ever possess in your business. The value is due to your pitch being the foundation for all the success you will enjoy in the future. All the money you'll ever spend in marketing, advertising and promotion will be based upon this pitch. If you're not getting the success you want, it's because of your pitch. It's not because of manufacturing issues, or people, or the latest trouble affecting the economy. It's because of your pitch. *If you invest in and perfect your pitch, your pitch will deliver for you.*

Exercise 2: Adding Emotion

Identify the Emotions Your Customers Experience from the Use of Your Product or Service

Instructions: Write in the **Product** or **Service Name** that you'll be describing in this exercise. Describe how your product or service brings your customers **Joy** or **Relief** using the template sentences below.

Exercise Time: 30min. List as many complete statements of Joy or Relief as you are able, from your customers' experience as a result of using your Product or Service. **Tip:** *Don't try to be Shakespere*, just get your thoughts on the paper— we'll refine these statements later.

Product or Service Name:

Benefit: **Benefit Category**

☐T ☐M ☐P ☐H ☐E ☐F

My customers feel (Joy or Relief Description)... _____

...as a result of (benefit explanation— from Section B, Exe. 1)... _____

...that allows them to (Benefit Category Type —from Exe. 1)... _____

...as a result of (Function or Process explanation —from Section C, Exe. 1)... _____

Benefit: **Benefit Category**

☐T ☐M ☐P ☐H ☐E ☐F

My customers feel (Joy or Relief Description)...

...as a result of (benefit explanation— from Section B, Exe. 1)...

...that allows them to (Benefit Category Type —from Exe. 1)...

...as a result of (Function or Process explanation —from Section C, Exe. 1)...

Benefit: **Benefit Category**

☐T ☐M ☐P ☐H ☐E ☐F

My customers feel (Joy or Relief Description)...

...as a result of (benefit explanation— from Section B, Exe. 1)...

...that allows them to (Benefit Category Type —from Exe. 1)...

...as a result of (Function or Process explanation —from Section C, Exe. 1)...

"Your pitch showcases your customer value—
make it memorable."

How to Incorporate Emotion into Your Pitch

If you're ever in doubt about the effectiveness of your pitch, ask yourself any of the following questions:

- What am I not understanding about my customers' viewpoints regarding my product?
- Have my customers' needs changed since introducing my product? If so, how?
- Are there new entrants in the marketplace competing for my customers? If so, how are they demonstrating their value and how does my pitch compare to theirs?

Here's the great news! Once you have the right pitch, everything flows. It's thrilling, and you're going to feel it. When you have the right pitch, your message is more easily explained and understood. As a result, any communication you produce to promote your product or service, based upon your pitch, is going to be more effective. This means advertisements built upon the pitch will connect more effectively. This translates into more engagement. This means more views and more conversions from an ad campaign. At trade shows, functions, or networking events, you'll easily engage far more people than you were able to do before your new pitch. If you attend conferences and normally have an hour to engage three people, the right pitch should be able to help you engage more people as a result. Why? Well for one, your pitch is much shorter. You won't need five or 10 minutes to communicate your pitch. You only need 10 seconds, and from there, you can determine if people are interested in you or not. In a conference or networking event, if you have a faster pitch, you can deliver it more clearly and can engage your prospects sooner, then you can determine their viability and whether you should be moving on to another prospect.

Incorporating emotion into a pitch is the most powerful way in which to engage your prospects and is the least used and understood approach in the sales pitching process. This means if you do it the right way, with care for your customer, and from a service-mindset, you are going to stand out. Because you've tied emotion and value into your pitch, you've created a powerful one-two punch in order to deliver meaningful value and engage the customers you desire.

By now it should be obvious how important it is for you to do these exercises. Take advantage of this opportunity and write as many possible emotional tie-ins to the value proposition as you can. You should have a page full of them.

Get started. Please don't move on to the next chapter until you've completed this exercise. You'll thank me later when we get to Chapter Five and we put it all together.

Behind every invitation is an opportunity to serve

Chapter Four:
The Invitation, Your Friendly Call to Action

I'm excited for you right now because you're close to completing your 3-Step Winning Pitch. The reason I'm excited is because I know your business is very likely to change for the better. You're going to have more confidence, increased effectiveness, and greater joy in your work life. Some people might say, "Hey, that's terrific!" but I know it goes a step further because if you have more joy and success in your work life, it will translate to more joy in your personal pursuits, your family life, and your ability to connect with the world around you. The techniques in this guide will likely help you in your daily personal communication—and that thrills me! This is the end goal of the 3-Step Winning Pitch Framework.

When you apply the framework, you'll be one of those shining-light kind of people who others look towards for inspiration and leadership. I hope you agree, that's a pretty cool place to be. But before we get all excited about it, it's time to conclude this exercise with the final part of the 3-Step Winning Pitch Framework, which is offering a friendly, invitational call to action.

Your call to action should embody a caring, service mindset—one that invites a loved one, a family member or a dear friend. It's essential for you to pitch from this mindset because it focuses on your interest of serving people rather than attempting to manipulate them. As long as you're focusing on a high level of service, you'll be remembered for caring for people rather than thinking about how uncomfortable it was to deal with you because of your manipulative tactics. It's counterintuitive that you want your pitch to not sound like a pitch. It's counterintuitive for you to want your close to not sound like a close, but it's the mindset you need to succeed. When writing your 10-second pitch, you must focus on service, not selling.

Obligatory Golf Analogy

If you've ever played golf, you know that excelling at the game is counterintuitive. If you're a beginner, you know this especially to be true. The whole logic when you start playing golf is to swing the clubhead as fast and with as much strength as you possibly can, because you'd expect that the harder you swing the clubhead, the farther distance the ball would travel. In reality, you want a relaxed swing. The best golfers in the world have a relaxed swing. You get more power when you relax into the swing than by forcing your swing. When you force your swing, the ball often doesn't go anywhere near your goal. Brute force doesn't work (at least not for beginners). To get the results you desire, you need to relax into your swing. It needs to feel natural and seemingly effortless—just like the pros. The same process applies to your pitch. *Your pitch should feel effortless and relaxed—never forced*. This requires that your call to action be presented in the form of an *invitation*.

Getting your "DeNiro Nod"

The call to action in the 3-Step Winning Pitch Framework often results in a physical clue or *"tell"* from your prospect that they're interested in listening to more about your offer. This means a nod, a forward lean, or some kind of physical sign that will help you determine if you're going to get permission (or not) to talk to them more about your product or service and perhaps engage in a product demo.

Pitchfreaks refer to this nod as a "DeNiro" after the actor, Robert DeNiro. Next time you watch DeNiro in a movie and see him agree with another character, watch his face and you'll instantly understand.

Fun Fact: there are several types of DeNiro nods, with each indicating a different level of interest. These include "Skeptical DeNiro", "Curious DeNiro", "Surprised DeNiro", and (The Ultimate) "Impressed DeNiro". See how many levels of DeNiros you can spot. Start paying attention in your pitches to see if you're getting a DeNiro.

Remember, no DeNiro—no *dinero!*

Clarity and Simplicity Leads to Action

Your call to action needs to be simple. It needs to be easy for your prospect to participate. It's critical that you engage in Steps One and Two of the 3-Step Winning Pitch Framework to make sure you've built appropriate trust and credibility with your prospect for a deeper conversation. If you did your job well—if your pitch is constructed in the right way, you're going to get your DeNiro nod.

> *There are only two reasons why people don't buy: 1. They don't see enough value in what you're offering. 2. You don't see enough value in what you're offering.*

This should be great news to you. Why? Because, should your prospect not be engaging with you during your presentation, you know it's for only one of two reasons, with each directly connected to your understanding and explanation of the value you're offering. Remember, the only perspective that matters is that of your customer. If you're not getting your DeNiros, go back to Step 1 and *rethink your value* from your customer's perspective.

The Mindset Behind Your Customer Invitation

I want you to think about how you typically invite loved ones or dear friends to events. You might also think about how you introduce friends or loved ones to try products you enjoy.

The third exercise will help you determine your ultimate "Call to Action" (CTA) for your specific sales communication. For those of you who have an aversion to selling or get uncomfortable with the sales process, this exercise will be especially helpful to you.

There's no conflict of interest when you're pitching to a loved one or a friend about a product or service you enjoy. You feel comfortable and relaxed in sharing something you feel confident about when you believe somebody else will derive some value from your recommendation. Why shouldn't you have the same feeling when pitching your product to your prospects?

Where there's no conflict of interest, you might say something like, "You've got to try this product, it's incredible!" or "I had the best time at this event." It's for this reason when you're pitching a prospect, you'll want to offer a friendly invitation to learn more about your offer rather than making a demand.

Prospects who are truly engaged want to be invited, they don't want to be demanded. It's a pull, not a push. Make sure you're inviting the prospect to learn a little bit more about your offer in whatever manner makes the most sense for your business.

If you happen to have a physical product, you can offer a sample, or you might say something like, "I have a sample I'd love to give you, if you're interested." If it's something you can actually show them, it would make it easy for them to understand what you're doing, you might say, "I have something to show you if you're interested", or, "I'd love to show it to you if you have a moment." or "I have a picture on my phone—I can show you if you have a moment?" or "If you have a moment, I could tell you more about it?"

"If you have a moment, I'd love to show you." is probably the most powerful call to action you can offer. It's simple, it's engaging, and it puts control into the hands of the prospect because you need them to make the decision to (hopefully) say, "Yes."

Exercise 3:
Offering a Customer Invitation (Call to Action)

Write as many casual, invitational Calls to Action that make sense for your business. Use the examples I've provided as a starting point. Use your own words. "I'd love to show you how I can deliver this result, if you have a moment." "If you have a moment, I'd love to offer you a sample." "If you think this may be a fit, I'd love to send you a link to the product on our website." "If this sounds interesting to you, I love to send you a text to get a free sample." "If you'd like, I'd love to drop a tester in the mail for you." "If you'd like to learn more, I'd love to give you my phone/email/etc." "We can hop on a video call if you're interested."

Caution: Avoid presumptive closes and manipulative techniques in your CTA. Your invitation should be genuine and from the heart, allowing your prospect to choose their acceptance of your invitation—freely and without guilt nor obligation. Remember, you are not closing the sale at this stage, you are earning the right to continue your presentation and engage the full attention of your prospect.

Now's your time to write down a list of possible calls to action in an invitational way that can work for your offer. Think about different situations you would experience (on the phone, in person, over a Video call, in a networking meeting, Intergalactic Telepathy)—whatever! Think about all the ways in which you react with customers or prospects to have a call to action make sense within the framework of whichever type of conversation you're having.

"A service-focused pitch will elevate you in the eyes of your customers."

Exercise 3: Invitational Call to Action
Make customers *feel invited* and welcomed *to learn more* about your offer

Instructions: Write 10 invitational calls to action that make sense for your specific product or service. Reference the examples provided below to get you started. Your encouraged to use your own words and personal communication style. **Exercise Time: 15min.** List as many invitational customer calls to action as you can. Remember, use the service mindset and aviod presumptive and manipulative closes. **Tip:** Your goal is to get another 10 seconds of your customers time so you can enter the next stage of your sales call.

Example Invitational Calls to Action

- I'd love to show you how this works, if you have a moment?
- I can send you a link to our website, if you're interested to get more information?
- I'd love to send you a sample, if you'd like to see for yourself?
- I'd love to hop on a video call with you so you can see this for yourself.
- I'd love to shoot you a text when we have a sample in stock for you to see.
- I'd love to show you how we can deliver these results if you've got a moment.

Write Your Own Invitational Closes

Invitation 1. _____

Invitation 2. _____

Invitation 3.

Invitation 4.

Invitation 5.

Invitation 6.

Invitation 7.

Invitation 8.

Invitation 9.

Invitation 10.

Invitation 11.

Selling is easier when your intention is to delight.

Chapter Five:
Putting It All Together

There are three important phases when making a movie, and creating a pitch is a lot like making a movie. The three phases of making a movie are: *pre-production*, *production*, and *post-production*. It's similar for novelists—you have an *outline*, then a *series of drafts* and then you have a *final manuscript*. The same holds true for your pitch.

Now that you have the results from the exercises in this book, namely: Exercise 1: *Identifying Your Value*; Exercise 2: *Adding Emotion*—such as joy or relief; and Exercise 3: *Creating an Invitational Call to Action*—now it's time to put them all together. You have done the pre-production work. Now it's time to get into production.

When you're filming a movie with many actors, you

might have many takes to get the performance you desire. One actor may not be speaking clearly or there might be a lighting glitch that needs fixing, or there may be any a number of things that might cause you to stop the action and re-shoot the scene.

The same concept applies in writing. If you're not sure you're conveying your idea in the best possible way, then you need write another draft. The whole idea is to create a very rough draft to get started. You need to get things down on paper to start connecting the dots. For many people this is where most of their self-doubt comes from, but since you've completed the previous exercises, you already have a solid foundation to work from.

It's time to get writing! Lights. Camera. *Action!*

Exercise 4: Complete Your 1st Draft

Reference your CWYO Exercise Guide download. Organize all your final choices into the Draft Pitch Organization Worksheet.

Part 1 - Final Selections from Exercise 1: Identifying Your Value: *Instructions* - Fill in the blanks from your final selections in Exercise 1

Part 2 - Final Selections from Exercise 2: Adding Emotions to Your Pitch: *Instructions* - Fill in the blanks from your final selections in Exercise 2

Part 3 - Final Selections from Exercise 3: Creating an Invitational Call to Action: *Instructions* - Write in your final sentence selection from Exercise 3

Part 4 - Create Your 1st Draft Pitch (Combine Parts 2 and 3 from the Exercise 4 worksheet): *Instructions* - From Part 2 and Part 3 of the worksheet, copy what you wrote in one complete paragraph to the complete 1st draft of your pitch.

Reminder: Fill in all three parts of the worksheet before moving on to Part 4, Your 1st Draft Pitch.

To complete your 1st Draft, you should have three complete sentences (a value sentence, an emotion sentence and an invitation sentence).

Don't Get Stuck: You're almost finished!

Here's the deal, many of us take on new projects, new educational programs, and we don't finish them. I've designed this book and these exercises to be easy to complete so you are more likely get the benefit from it. Write your draft, even if it's rough, even if it's messy, even if it makes no sense to begin with. Keep the faith, keep writing and it will eventually make sense for you. Don't worry if it doesn't sound articulate, don't worry if it doesn't sound engaging– just put the sentences together. You can do it! Once you complete this, we'll have the ultimate block of clay to work your final pitch in the final exercise (Exercise 5). There, you can shape the pitch however you want.

Putting It All Together

To help you along, try 3/3/3

From Exercise 1 (Value), pick three words that convey the entire meaning of the value proposition from the perspective of your customers. What are the three key words that are absolutely essential to convey this idea? Write them down. Now come up with the three words from Exercise 2 (Emotion) that articulate the emotion that is derived as a result of having used the product.

Finally, what are the three words from Exercise 3 (Invitation) in your casual, invitational call to action that are essential to complete the pitch? When you're finished, you should have nine words. Those nine words might not construct a sentence, but they'll make it easier to create your three sentences. When you deconstruct the overall description into these nine words, you can add words to build up to your pitch's 30 word limit. All you need to do is come up with the right words and make them into an intelligible sentence. Go ahead and try it now.

The 1/1/1

If 3/3/3 doesn't work, then pick one word per section. What's the one word that describes the value? What's the one value word that connects to a feature or function of your product? You cannot talk about more than one feature or benefit of your product in a 10-second pitch. You have to pick the best (according to your customers' needs). You have to pick the one that's going to excite your prospect the most. If you can't simplify what you pitch, then you're going to continue to struggle. I encourage you to take advantage of this opportunity with this assignment and just pick a word to start. If it doesn't work, you can always pick an alternative and go through the exercise again. Pick one word and then build from there if you're having trouble.

In 10 Seconds, you can only focus on one benefit and one function. Within this constraint is freedom.

If you're having a hard time refining and reducing the words, remember— you only have 10 seconds to communicate this idea. Therefore, you can only communicate the one function of your product or service that is special. You can only communicate one emotional benefit that ties into the function of the product. And you can only have one invitation (call to action). This is where a lot of people have difficulty. They have a hard time choosing the priority regarding their customers. In reality, it's a matter of prioritizing what's most important for your business.

Exercise 4: Complete your 1st Draft Pitch

It's time to *Commit to Your Pitch,* with this easy to use *Draft Pitch Organization Worksheet*

Instructions: Fill in the blanks for Parts 1 through 4 below, using the descriptions and explanations you made previously from the last three exercises. **Exercise Time: 30min. Tip:** Do not over complicate this, simply fill in the blanks, in order—step-by-step, and you'll see your pitch *magically* begin to reveal.

Part 1
Final Selections From Exercise 1: Identifying Your Value
Instructions: Fill in the blanks from your final selections in **Exercise 1**

1. *Final Benefit Selection:*
Write your final choice from **Exercise 1, Section A…**

_____

_____

_____

2. *Final Explanation Selection:*
Write your final choice from **Exercise 1, Section B…**

_____

_____

_____

3. *Final Function/Process Selection:*
Write your final choice from **Exercise 1, Section C…**

_____

_____

_____

Part 2
Final Selections From Exercise 2: Adding Emotion
Instructions: Fill in the blanks from your final selections in **Exercise 2**

---

4. My Customers feel _____ as a
                                         (Joy or Relief Description)

result of _____
          (Final Benefit Explanation)

_____ that allows

them to _____
        (Final Benefit Category Description)

_____ thanks

to _____
   (Final Final Function or Process Description)

_____ .

Part 3
Final Selections From Exercise 3: Invitational Call to Action
Instructions: Write in your final sentence selection from Exercise 3

---

5. _____

_____

_____

_____

Part 4
Create Your 1st Draft Pitch (Combine Part 2 and Part 3)
Instructions: From Part 2 and Part 3 of this exercise, copy what you wrote in one complete paragraph below to complete the 1st draft of your pitch.

"Your pitch is a sprint—
make sure your offer is in shape."

Exercise 5: Writing Your Final Draft

Now that you have your three sentences together, I want you to do a word count. If you are able, write the draft using a word processor. If it's written on paper, count the total words. How many words do you have in your statement? Once you have your first word count, that's where the fun begins!

The Final 30

Your word count should be 30 words. That's right, 30 words. You might be looking at 300 words or 3,000 words right now, and that's okay.

The goal here is to reduce your pitch down to 30 words, because that is the number of words you can speak in 10 seconds without sounding rushed and pressured. It's the 10 seconds referred to at the beginning of this book. If you want to get somebody engaged with your pitch, then your job is to edit your sentences down to 30 words so you can deliver your 10-second pitch in a relaxed and confident manner. While a great pitch requires 10 seconds, I've had epic pitches comprised of fewer than 10 words and deliverable in less than 10 seconds. You're not required to make a 10-second pitch if you can do it less time.

If you recall from the YouTube example, some people abandoned a video within two and a half seconds after clicking on a thumbnail. This means you could have as few as two and a half seconds to connect with a prospect.

If you're having trouble cutting down to 30 words, focus on the product or service function— that singular function providing the most relevant value, while also bringing you the most profit.

Pitchfreaks focus on high margin selling strategies. We are focused on premium offerings within our industries. There's no point in investing time and money in a pitch that's not profitable. If you're in business, you should have a plan on how to make money. If you care about being a successful businessperson, then you should be laser-focused on getting great profit margins. The whole point of the 3-Step Winning Pitch Framework is to gain more credibility, more trust, and ultimately a higher profit margin.

Having your completed 10-second pitch means your intentions are clear and that you understand the needs of your customers. Your pitch is the most powerful tool with which you conduct your business.

What does this mean? It means that the words in those first ten seconds should be the words that are music to your prospect's ears. It should be words to build trust in you and to know that your offering is right for them. Those should be the very first words in your pitch.

You want to make sure you front-load your 10-second statement (your first 30 words) with the most important, compelling words, the words your customers care about most. One of my favorite pitches was for a company in the construction business that was less than 10 words, but those few words helped the company turn around during the economic crisis of 2008—taking them from a very deep financial hole, to thriving and generating millions of dollars in sales for 12 years, as of the time of this writing. You don't need 30 words if 10 words will do.

"Do not complicate things. Only do as much as is needed to achieve your objective as quickly as possible."
— *Bruce Lee*

The challenge for most people is simplifying their communication. The exercise of using three words to represent the value, three words to represent the emotion, and three words to represent the invitation, is designed to help you reduce your word count.

Your 10 Second Sprint!

Great! You now have your 30 words.

The challenge to having more than 30 words in your pitch is that you won't be able to convey your idea in a relaxed, confident matter within 10 seconds. The 3-Step Winning Pitch Framework is designed to imbue you and your presentation with credibility, authority, and trust. 30 words is the outer limit to be able to communicate an idea comfortably and with confidence.

Don't try 31 or 35 words. It doesn't work, *because you'll have to speak too fast* to deliver your 10 second pitch. You don't want to be perceived as some kind of a fast-talking hustler.

Now that you have the framework and the rules of

this particular game, you can start playing with the way in which you construct your final words, and you can choose whichever functions or features you want. Put them together in any combination that allows you to deliver the pitch in a comfortable, confident, and relaxed manner.

When you complete your 10-second pitch, getting it down to fewer than 30 words or less, I want you to email it to me: pitch@pitchfreaks.com. I have a gift that I want to send to you as a thank you for executing these assignments and investing in your future.

The 3-Step Winning Pitch Framework is going to help you reveal who you are to those whom you wish to serve. It's going to help you connect. It's going to help you build trust. It's going to help you build engagement. It's going to help you improve your life and those of your customers.

Exercise 5: Refine Your Final Pitch
Get to your final pitch by refining several drafts with this Pitch Draft Editing Worksheet

Instructions: Fill in the blanks in Parts 1 through 3 below, using the selections you made previously in the past three exercises. **Exercise Time: 30min. Tip:** The end of this exercise is your final pitch, so make sure each draft you create expresses your value, connects more emotionally, and delivers an invitation that gets your *"DeNiro Nod"*.

Refine Your Pitch:
Review and copy your pitch from your final selections in Exercise 4 and write it down below. Fix any obvious spelling and/or grammar as needed.

_____

_____
_____
_____
_____
_____
_____
_____
_____
_____
_____
_____

1st Draft Word Count _____ (note: your final count MUST be no more than 30 words) Is your paragraph word count 30 words or less? If yes, congratulations, you're now ready to have a colleague or trusted friend proofread and comment on your pitch. If your word count is above 30 words, please rewrite your pitch below with fewer words to meet the Pitchfreak's 30 word limit requirement.

2nd Draft Pitch: Refine your 1st Draft and reduce your word count to 30 words or less.

___

2nd Draft Word Count _____ If your word count is above 30 words, rewrite to meet the Pitchfreak's 30 word limit requirement.

3rd Draft Pitch: Refine your 2nd Draft and reduce your word count to 30 words or less.

___

3rd Draft Word Count _____ If your word count is above 30 words, rewrite to meet the Pitchfreak's 30 word limit requirement.

My Open

Congratulations!

Welcome to your Final Pitch!

In the space provided below, write down your 3rd Draft, 30 Word Pitch, and reduce it to 30 words or fewer, to complete your Final Pitch!

You did it! You're now ready to have a colleague or trusted friend proofread and comment on your pitch. If your pitch is 30 words or less, you're entitled to a free pitch analysis. Simply email your final pitch to us at pitch@pitchfreaks.com - *Congratulations, again!*

*"You made it! May your dreams guide
you to amazing adventures."*

Always Pitch from the Service Mindset

As long as you're focused on the service mindset and providing value—which is the core tenant of the 3-Step Winning Pitch Framework—you're going to win. It may take time. It may take a lot of practice, but ultimately you will prevail.

Don't give up. Keep fighting. Do the work.

Congratulations! Bravo! You made it! Now go forth and pitch, fellow Pitchfreak!

May your actions always be up the challenge of your dreams.

If you'd like to share your experience and collaborate with Pitchfreaks from around the world, we'd love to have you join our community at www.Pitchfreaks.com. Come join the fun!

Keep Pitching!
Your pal, the Pitchfreak!

Antonio White
San Francisco, CA

Afterword

Congratulations! You've got your 3-Step Winning Pitch. You did it! I am excited for you! Now it's time for you to rock and roll.

Here's what you're going to do. You're going to start rehearsing this pitch and presenting it to as many people as possible. You want to role play with people from your company, family members, past customers, existing customers, anybody you can talk to who will listen and allow you to practice your pitch. There are only two critical components to a pitch, the *content* and your *delivery*. Now that you have the content, you must put equal effort into developing the quality of your delivery. That means practicing your pitch and performing it with people you trust BEFORE you present it in a real-life sales event. When you practice your pitch, it's not for people to give their personal comments, but rather to address any confusion that may exist in your pitch. People can offer you basic, grammatical constructive comments to help you improve, but your practice sessions are not an invitation for people (except for trusted professional peers) to give you their opinion of your strategy, or business, or marketing, etc. Be open minded to ideas that help make your pitch stronger and avoid ideas that add distraction or vagueness. A Pitchfreaks pitch should be engaging—never boring!

Every Top Performer Needs to Train

You should practice your pitch and train regularly, just like an athlete. Even top performing athletes are required to train regularly before they're allowed on the playing field. Just like an actor has to rehearse before they can take the stage, you also need to rehearse and perfect your pitch in a safe place, a place where you can receive support to make sure you're communicating with the intention you desire before you make your pitch in front of a real prospect.

One of the biggest weakness I find in people's pitches is inadequate practice. They have not rehearsed their pitch enough. They don't role-play enough to make sure their pitch is delivered naturally when they get in front of a prospect.

Practice Your Pitches with Fellow Pitchfreaks

Since you've completed all the included exercises and have created your 30-word pitch, you are now officially a Pitchfreak! As a result, you've got benefits coming. The first, being a place where you can meet fellow Pitchfreaks and practice your new pitch. To help you in this endeavor, we created an online community where you're invited to join— www.Pitchfreaks.com.

The community helps support you and your fellow Pitchfreaks who are going through the process of practicing their pitches. You can practice your pitches along with other professionals in multiple industries who have taken the same training course as you and can give you constructive feedback in a safe place where you can practice and be more effective when you get in front of an actual prospect.

To get access to this free online community of professionals, simply go to www.Pitchfreaks.com and subscribe to the Pitchfreaks Private Community Group. You'll be asked to register, and of course you'll be asked to submit your 3-Step Winning Pitch (30 words or less). Once we receive and review your pitch, we'll send you a link to gain access to our online role-playing, coaching, and training programs along with invitations to join fun events.

Getting my pitch right has made a profound, meaningful, and positive impact on my life. As a result of getting my pitch right, my business has blossomed. My personal relationships have increased dramatically with greater trust, greater insights, and greater love.

Thank you for being a Pitchfreak. Thank you for participating in this process. Let us know how we can help. Email "support@pitchfreaks.com". Visit our website and learn more about how you can participate in our community at www.Pitchfreaks.com.

Come join us to support your continued development!

Acknowledgments

First and foremost, *thank you* for buying this book.

This project would not be possible without the support of my wife, editor and designer, Christina Z. White.

Thank you to all my teachers, especially Ronnie Simpson, John Parish, Floyd Glenn, and Marsha Pannone. Thanks Hon. Willie L. Brown, Jr. for my first ad campaign at 18 years old. Thank you, Ivo Cardelli for my first job in design. Thank you, Eric, for my first gig as a graphic designer at West Coast Beauty Supply *(Hi to Joseph, Calvin and Rosa)*. Thanks, John Skinner of Canon Press for my first office space (for *free*). Thank you, Tony Masood. Thanks, Mann Brothers (Harold and Alex), Modern Media Ventures, Red Dot Interactive, and Irene Graff. Thank you, Tammy, for the early days and to my Digital Deli crew: Brian Lee Thomas, Raul Visceral, Chef John Mitzewich, and Consuelo Dela Rosa. Thanks also to Stephen, Tyrone "Big T" Woods, Sara, Marc, Ryan, Brad Suskind, and Raquel Garcia. Thank you, Gwendolyn and Marco Sanchez. Thank you, Paul, Toni-lynn, Katrina, Peter and Mary Chetirkin. Special thanks to my Silicon Valley marketing pals: AJ Brown, Ram Srinivasan, Shaw Taylor, Theresa Marcroft, John Stallcup, Steve O'Brien, Sandeep Jain, Eric J. Archembeau, Perry Mizota, Nadine Wolff, Melissa Horwath, Kellie Menendez, Laura Moreno Lucas, Liz Curtis, and the brilliant Scott Eagle. Much love and thanks to Donna Jean "FreakyD" McIntyre. Thank you, Nicole Carpenter, Kathy Lane, JeffTheEntrepreneur, CrazyJerr, Emanuel Svechinsky, Coach Ken Joslin, Mikey C-Roc, Carolyn Flowers, Sherri Innis, and Salana and Del Whitehead. Heartfelt thanks to Grant Cardone, Brandon Dawson, Billy Gene, Brian Rose, Damon John, John Taffer, Scott Dickers, Kelly Cullen, Don Falk, Terry Sellards, Sam Singer, Piero Patri, Cindi Testa-McCullagh, Bert Hill, J.J. Panzer, Joel Panzer, Jaclyn Carpenter, Gayle Gaggler, Judy Venheisen, Martin Cooper, Dr. Peter Rabanus, Dr. Orlo Clarke, Dr. Robert Allen, Craig Newmark, MajGen Mike Myatt, Wilkes Bashford, Pete Ratto, Patricia Fripp, Dennis Minnick, Myron S. Eichen, Ray Siotto and *The* Sidney Mobell. Thank you pioneers: Steve Jobs, David Ogilvy, Stephen Covey, Mahan Khalsa, Miyamoto Musashi, Bruce Lee, Stan Lee, Zig Ziglar, Eckhart Tolle, Wayne Dyer, Scott McCloud, Harvey McKay, Paul Rand, Rex Ray, Jennifer Morla, Gary Vaynerchuck, April Greiman and Derral Eves. The Architects: Walter Landor, Regis McKenna, Claude C. Hopkins, John Caples, Stephen King, Primo Angeli, Ken McCarthy, *The* Gary Halburt, Prof. George Lakoff and *The* Joel Bauer. Thank you, Grandparents, Estanislao, Carmen, Vera, and John. Thank you to my merchandising genius Mother, Emily; to my photographer Super-Bro! John D. White; and lastly, thank you to my "Pop", Serge, who shared with me his love of entrepreneurship (I miss you every day).

About the Author

The origins of the Pitchfreak, Antonio White, began as a painfully shy little boy exposed to gamma-radiation-like ink marker fumes while doodling in school and gained freak-like superpowers of graphic persuasion. What started out as a way to emotionally connect with people through art, turned into a career helping high-tech innovators make millions through successful investor and new product launch pitches. From M&As to IPOs—the young David Ogilvy disciple—led a quiet life as a creative hired gun for Venture funded startups. The Pitchfreak created investor and/or new product introduction pitches for NASA, UCSF, NBC, Brøderbund, Quantum, Cisco, Sagent, Datamind, Portivity, Fireclick, Personic, Claria, Viquity, Tavolo and many others. After 25 years of crafting pitches and over $750M in sales exits, the Pitchfreak loves transferring his winning pitch strategies and tactics to a new generation of effective entrepreneurs and ambitious, driven startup founders.

You can learn more about pitching and the Pitchfreaks Community at www.Pitchfreaks.com.

Printed in Great Britain
by Amazon